For Barbara and Bob—
with love—
Bernie
June 1998

PARTICIPATING IN GOVERNMENT:

OPPORTUNITIES TO VOLUNTEER

by Bernard Ryan, Jr.

Ryan, Bernard, 1923-
    Community service for teens: opportunities to volunteer / Bernard
Ryan, Jr.
      p. cm.
  Includes bibliographical references and index.
  Contents: [1] Caring for animals -- [2] Expanding education and
literacy -- [3] Helping the ill, the poor & the elderly -- [4] Increasing
neighborhood service -- [5] Participating in government --
- -[6] Promoting the arts and sciences -- [7] Protecting the environment
- -[8] Serving with police, fire & EMS
    ISBN 0-89434-227-4 (v. 1). -- ISBN 0-89434-231-2 (v. 2). -- ISBN
0-89434-229-0 (v. 3). -- ISBN 0-89434-233-9 (v. 4). --
ISBN 0-89434-230-4 (v. 5). -- ISBN 0-89434-234-7 (v. 6). --
ISBN 0-89434-228-2 (v. 7). -- ISBN 0-89434-232-0 (v. 8)
    1. Voluntarism—United States—Juvenile literature. 2. Young
volunteers—United States—Juvenile literature. 3. Teenage
volunteers in social service—United States—Juvenile literature.
[1. Voluntarism.] I. Title.
HN90.V64R93 1998
361.3'7'08350973—dc21   97-34971
                                                                                        CIP
                                                                                        AC

Community Service for Teens: Participating in Government:
Opportunities to Volunteer

A New England Publishing Associates Book
Copyright ©1998 by Ferguson Publishing Company
ISBN 0-89434-230-4

Published and distributed by
Ferguson Publishing Company
200 West Madison, Suite 300
Chicago, Illinois 60606
800-306-9941
Web Site: http://www.fergpubco.com

Printed in the United States of America
V-3

CONTENTS

INTRODUCTION

Six out of ten American teenagers work as volunteers. A 1996 survey revealed that the total number of teen volunteers aged 12 to 17 is 13.3 million. They give 2.4 billion hours each year. Of that time, 1.8 billion hours are spent in "formal" commitments to nonprofit organizations. Informal help, like "just helping neighbors," receives 600 million hours.

Each "formal" volunteer gives an average of three and a half hours a week. It would take nearly 1.1 million full-time employees to match these hours. And if the formal volunteers were paid minimum wage for their time, the cost would come to at least $7.7 billion—a tremendous saving to nonprofit organizations.

Teen volunteerism is growing. In the four years between the 1996 survey and a previous one, the number of volunteers grew by 7 percent and their hours increased by 17 percent.

Equal numbers of girls and boys give their time to volunteering.

How voluntary is volunteering? Only 16 out of 100 volunteers go to schools that insist on community service before graduation. Twenty-six out of 100 are in schools that offer courses requiring community service if you want credit for the course.

Six out of ten teen volunteers started volunteering before they were 14 years old. Seventy-eight percent of teens who volunteer have parents who volunteer.

Only 16 out of 100 volunteers go to schools that insist on community service before graduation.

WHY VOLUNTEER?

When teens are asked to volunteer, the 1996 survey revealed, nine out of ten do so. Who does the asking? Usually a friend, teacher, relative or church member. Teens gave a number of reasons for volunteering, regardless of whether their schools required community service. Their reasons included:

- You feel compassion for people in need.
- You feel you can do something for a cause that is important to you.
- You believe that if you help others, others will help you.
- Your volunteering is important to people you respect.
- You learn to relate to others who may be different from you.
- You develop leadership skills.
- You become more patient.
- You gain a better understanding of good citizenship.
- You get a chance to learn about various careers.
- You gain experience that can help in school and can lead to college admission and college scholarships as well as future careers.

VOLUNTEER FOR WHAT?

You can volunteer in a wide variety of activities. To get a picture of how teen volunteering is spread among various categories, see Exhibit 1 on page 7.

Don't miss an opportunity that is disguised as a requirement.

—Karl Methven, Faculty Member and Head Coach, addressing the Class of 1997, Proctor Academy, Andover, New Hampshire, at the graduation ceremony May 31, 1997

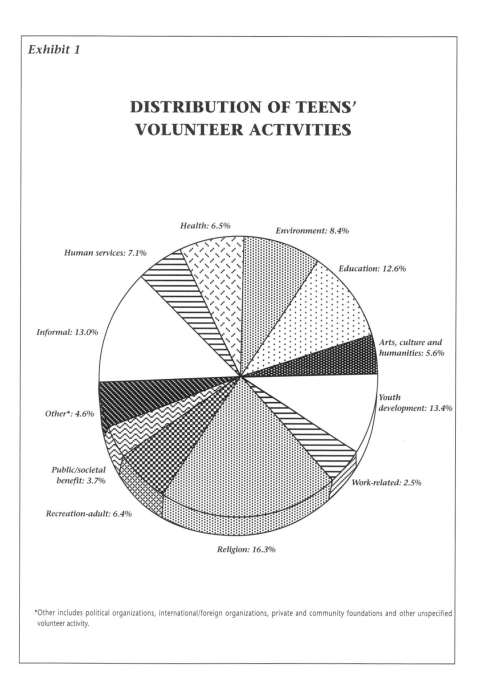

Exhibit 1

DISTRIBUTION OF TEENS'
VOLUNTEER ACTIVITIES

Health: 6.5%

Environment: 8.4%

Human services: 7.1%

Education: 12.6%

Informal: 13.0%

Arts, culture and
humanities: 5.6%

Youth
development: 13.4%

Other*: 4.6%

Public/societal
benefit: 3.7%

Work-related: 2.5%

Recreation-adult: 6.4%

Religion: 16.3%

*Other includes political organizations, international/foreign organizations, private and community foundations and other unspecified
volunteer activity.

(Source: <u>Volunteering and Giving Among American Teenagers: 1996.</u> Independent Sector, Washington,
DC, 1997.)

WHO SAYS YOU HAVE TO "VOLUNTEER"?

Is "volunteering" for community service required in your school? It is if you live in the state of Maryland or in the city of Atlanta, Georgia. In fact, in many school districts across the United States you cannot receive your high school diploma unless you have spent a certain number of hours in community service. The number of hours varies.

Who makes the rule? In Maryland, the only state so far to require every high school student to perform community service, it is the Maryland State Department of Education. In most school districts, it is the board of education, which usually sets policies that meet the standards of the community.

If you have to do it, is it voluntary? And is it legal to make you do it? One family didn't think so. In 1994, the parents of Daniel Immediato, a 17-year-old senior at Rye Neck High School in Mamaroneck, New York, sued in federal court to keep Daniel's school from requiring him to spend 40 hours in community service before he could graduate.

Daniel's parents said the requirement interfered with their right to raise their child, that it violated Daniel's privacy rights, and that it was a violation of the Thirteenth Amendment to the U.S. Constitution. That amendment says:

> Neither slavery nor involuntary servitude, except as a punishment for a crime whereof the party shall have been duly convicted, shall exist within the United States, or any place subject to their jurisdiction.

(Continued on page 9)

8

(Continued from page 8)

The requirement for community service, said the Immediatos, imposed involuntary servitude on Daniel.

In its defense, the Rye Neck School Board argued that what it wanted was to get the students out into the community to see what goes on in the outside world. In the process, said the board, students would find out what it was like to have to dress appropriately for a job, be on time somewhere and have other people dependent on them. The emphasis was not on what the community would gain, it was on what the student would learn.

The court decided the school system was right. The Immediatos appealed. The U.S. Court of Appeals for the Second Circuit upheld the decision. The Immediatos asked the U.S. Supreme Court to hear the case. It turned down the request, as it does many appeals, without stating its reason for refusing.

"If schools are going to demand that volunteering be part of success as a teenager," says Susan Trafford, president, Habitat for Humanity, Central Westmoreland, Pennsylvania, "I think the teens need to have, first, a selection in the volunteerism that they are going to do, and second, an understanding that this is a responsibility. This is the real world. This isn't the high school. This isn't the halls of Central High. I don't think we can just send them off and say, 'Now, here's your volunteer day.' They need a cause to go there, an understanding of someone, of what they will be contributing to. Sure, there are wonderful things that can be done. But don't send me six who have to do this before they can graduate."

What Is Government?

*Y*ou have been aware of some kind of government almost from the day you were born. Just being in a family means you know something about government. Someone makes the rules and decisions that affect how everyone behaves, and someone enforces the rules. That is true not only in a family but also in any organization beyond the family, whether a private club, Little League team, school or business.

GOVERNMENT: MANY SIZES, MANY FORMS

Usually, however, when you think of government you think of a more public organization that has power over everyone within a certain geographic area. It may be the government of a village, town, city, county, state or nation.

However large or small a government is, it includes several components:

- *Rules.* No group, whether as small as a family or as large as a nation, can function if it does not set rules of conduct. Rules determine how the behavior of individuals affects the entire group. Some behavior is favored or required; some is discouraged or prohibited.

- *Authority.* Every government has to get its power from somewhere. Down through history, power often came from individuals, such as kings and emperors. Even today, in some countries, individuals hold absolute authority as dictators. But in democratic countries, such as the United States, authority lies with the body of citizens—that is, the people.
- *Legality.* What establishes that authority in a democracy? A body of laws approved by the body of citizens. When the people of a democratic country accept the authority of their government, they put laws in place that both empower and limit the government. The body of laws makes the government legitimate.
- *Jurisdiction.* This word answers the question of control: *Where* does the government have authority, on *what* issues and over *whom?* If you live within the geographic area over which a public government—national, state, county, city, town or village—has authority, you are within that government's jurisdiction. You must accept its laws or move somewhere else.

   The jurisdiction of public government in the United States covers many aspects of our lives. For example, it covers education, taxation, social welfare, marriage and divorce, business and professional activity, transportation, the economy and public health.
- *Enforcement.* There is no point in setting up rules unless they are enforced. Most people accept the rules made by their governments at each level from local to national, but some choose not to. Systems are put in place that insist on behavior that comes within the rules and that correct or punish behavior that is outside the rules.

In democratic countries, such as the United States, authority lies with the body of citizens—that is, the people.

THREE LEVELS OF GOVERNMENT

Who does *what* at different levels of government?

At *local* levels—cities, counties, towns and villages—you will find government running:

- schools
- fire departments
- police departments
- emergency medical services (EMS)
- libraries
- services for the elderly
- planning and zoning (building permits)
- public works (water, sewage, refuse collection, recycling)
- mass transportation (buses, subways)

At the *state* level, government is responsible for:

- standards of education
- colleges and universities
- public safety (state police)
- public health (disease control)
- social welfare
- environmental conservation
- licensing businesses and professions

At the *national* level, the federal government handles many functions, including:

- printing and coining money
- international relations
- delivery of mail
- defense and warfare
- regulation of transportation, communications, trade and commerce
- Social Security and general welfare

At *all* levels, the various governments handle legislation, courts, taxation, parks and recreation, and the construction and repair of roads and highways.

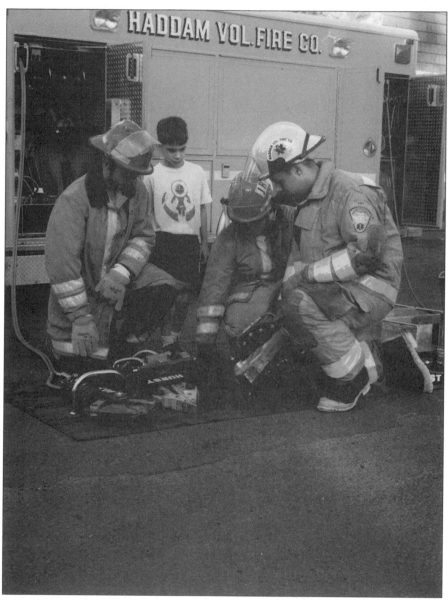

(V. Harlow/Haddam Volunteer Fire Company, Haddam, CT)

Local governments are in charge of running various schools, commissions and departments. In Haddam, Connecticut, the fire department is composed entirely of volunteers and controlled by Haddam's Board of Selectmen.

GOVERNMENT: MANY JOBS, MANY PEOPLE

Across America, some 22 million people work in government. That's about 1 out of every 7 civilians. Of those, about 3 million work for the federal government, *not* including military service. In fact, the largest employer in our country is the U.S. government. Why? Simply because it takes all those people to perform the many services that our national government provides. The other 19 million government workers fill jobs at every level from the state down to the village.

▼

Across America, some 22 million people work in government.

You may be thinking about a career in government. Perhaps that is one reason why you are reading this book and considering spending some volunteer time in this field. You can be in almost any line of work and find a career in government. Engineers, doctors, lawyers, scientists, educators, mechanics, carpenters, masons, computer programmers, personnel experts (often known as human resource people), stenographers, space explorers, weather forecasters, air traffic controllers—the list goes on and on.

Why work in government? It may sound idealistic, but you do serve the people when you work for them, at every level from local to national. The pay is reasonably good—about even with pay in the private sector. If you're doing a good job, you can be promoted to more responsibility fairly quickly. And typically you get excellent vacation and retirement benefits as well as low-cost health and life insurance coverage.

As the following chapters will tell you, volunteers are welcomed in many government offices and at all levels. Not all have places for teenagers, but—as you will see—some have discovered how valuable teen volunteer time and effort can be for them. And many have set up intern opportunities for college students, who come into a government agency for a semester or even a year, or for an intensive two or three weeks during a spring break, to see how they like it.

(Courtesy: Bill Jones, secretary of state, Sacramento, CA)

There are many government offices throughout the United States who welcome teenage volunteers. Bill Jones, secretary of state in California, speaks with one of his interns, Scott Jones, about a recent office project.

WHERE DOES POLITICS FIT IN?

In a democracy, it's impossible to entirely separate politics from government. If we did, it wouldn't be a democracy anymore because politics is the means by which citizens keep control over government and influence its policies.

We depend on political parties to gain and keep control of governments. Political parties are groups of people who are like-minded or have broadly similar points of view. The groups or parties compete with each other, each trying to make its point of view predominant over the opposition's. The parties nominate candidates to run for various elective offices in government, and work to get their candidates elected. Traditionally in America, we have depended on a *two-party system*—that is, with only two parties dividing the vast majority of the voting population—but occasionally a third party has been strong enough to become a factor in an election.

The system becomes unwieldy if every citizen has a direct voice in every decision.

In any area larger than a small community such as a village or town, the system becomes unwieldy if every citizen has a direct voice in every decision that is to be made by the government. So we have a system called *representative democracy.* The citizens nominate and elect people to represent them in the government, and the representatives make the laws and enforce them.

These groups of representatives go by various names. In small towns (particularly in the New England states), this body is called the "board of selectmen." In cities of all sizes, even as large as New York City, you will find a "city council." At the state level, there is a legislature usually comprising two bodies: the "assembly" (called the "House of Representatives" in many states) and the "Senate." And nationally we have the "United States Congress," comprising the "House of Representatives" and the "Senate."

At all of these levels, usually one political party's representatives are dominant, holding the majority of votes. The other party, which is in the minority and thus "out of power," works hard to provide criticism of the party in power and to offer alternative policies and programs for the legislative body to consider.

(U.S. Senate photograph)

House Speaker Tip O'Neill (right) with President Gerald Ford in 1973.

"ALL POLITICS IS LOCAL"

The late "Tip" O'Neill, speaker of the U.S. House of Representatives, said, "All politics is local." It begins in each of the 146,300 election precincts in the United States. The organization works its way up to various levels: wards or districts, which include a number of precincts; cities, which include wards or districts; and counties,

17

with usually more than one town or city included. In turn, the county organizations reach up to the state level. In almost all cases, the two-party system is at work at each level, nominating candidates for various offices and working to get them elected.

You may or may not be interested in a career in politics itself— that is, in running for elective office some day. (It is not the aim of this book to describe or make a case for any political party.) But you may be interested in *political science,* which is the study of political life. This field is closely related to, if not a part of, the study of government. It encompasses many areas and activities, such as particular actions of a government (at any level), the push of pressure groups to put across their points of view, the various forces that influence election results, and the administration of public policy after it has been set by a legislative body.

A number of professional fields come together under the umbrella of political science. As a political scientist, you may specialize in any of these fields:

- *Political theory and history.* Based on studies of how political power has been won through the centuries, as well as how it has been lost, this is the philosophical area. It examines the minds and theories of each political giant from Plato in ancient Greece to Karl Marx in the 19th century and from Franklin Roosevelt to Ronald Reagan in the 20th century.
- *Comparative government.* Here you study the political customs of various countries to gain an understanding of political reality and see what works in one system that may be useful in another.
- *International relations.* This takes you into diplomacy and all the give-and-take that is always going on around the world. It encompasses the great forces of nationalism and imperialism that have clashed during the 19th and 20th centuries as well

as the more recent role of the United Nations and other multinational organizations. Today, trade and the environment are hot topics in international relations.

- *American government.* Concentrating here, you can gain a solid understanding of our systems of government at every level including the various federal agencies as well as the interest groups and mass media that have the skills and the strength to influence them.

- *Public administration.* Here you learn how things get done after government has set certain policies. Again, local, state and national levels are important, as government departments at each level must be made to perform effectively—even when (as may be the case at any level) there is political opposition that hinders the effort.

- *Political behavior.* What makes voters pick one candidate over another? The way one parts his hair? The way another wrinkles her nose? The sound of a voice? The answer to a question thrown from the crowd—or from the swarms of media people? How people respond to politicians or to political conditions is an area that can capture your attention and hold it for a long time.

Altogether, then, political science is a field of study that can give you an understanding of how government has evolved over the centuries and where it has been successful or has failed. By volunteering in any area of government, from local to national, you can become something of a political scientist. All you have to do is keep your eyes and ears open and use the opportunities you get to meet and listen to the people who elect and appoint their governments—as well as to those who are elected and appointed.

In the chapters that follow, you will read about a number of organizations and offices. Many projects and programs will be described, and you will learn from many individuals, both teens and adults who work with teens. Bear in mind that all the places, projects and people are included as *examples* of what is out there. No two are exactly alike. Most are typical. Some are unusual. But by learning about them, you will find out what kinds of volunteer opportunities may be waiting for you and whether similar opportunities would appeal to you.

What You'll Do as a Volunteer

*T*he type of work you can do as a volunteer in government and politics varies widely. You may help the busy staff of an elected official, such as your local mayor, a member of the city council, or a representative from your district or area who serves in your state's legislature or in Congress. You may help a nonpartisan group that is working to increase the registration of eligible voters and the understanding of the importance of voting. If you live in or near your state capital, you may help in your state's executive offices there.

Your help as a volunteer is vitally important in all the areas you are going to read about. Elected representatives and other officials in government almost never have enough help to handle the tremendous volume of calls, complaints, requests and demands that come in by phone, e-mail and the regular mail. Their staff people seldom enjoy a simple 9-to-5 day.

In some of the volunteer work you will be reading about, you can start as young as 12 or 13. In others, you may need to be 16 and have your driver's license.

LOCAL GOVERNMENT: MAYOR AND CITY COUNCIL

Suppose you are a teen volunteer in the office of a member of a city council. What will you be doing? Let Vincene Jones, secretary to city council member Sam Pannell in Sacramento, California, answer that question.

"I teach volunteers basically 95 percent of the work that I do," says Jones. "The only thing they cannot do for me is the scheduling. There have been times when I haven't been at work and they have handled the whole office—they just run my desk. They don't just come in and file. Filing is the lowest job on the totem pole. They file when there's absolutely nothing else to do."

In an office like this, you may find yourself handling any number of tasks each day. One of the most important is sorting the mail, to make sure that every incoming letter goes promptly to the council member who is responsible for the particular subject of the letter. Another key responsibility is answering constituents' telephone calls with courtesy and authority. You can't sound vague or uninformed when taking incoming calls.

Another duty is escorting visitors who have appointments into the office of the council member. Then there's research. You may be asked to find information on a given topic by calling or going to other departments of the city government or to the library.

That's not all. Jones says the teens help the administrative assistants in handling complaints from constituents and sending answers back as to what happened. They also help with special events. "The council member I work for is very active," she notes. "We have events all through the year. One we call Santa Sam, where we feed 300 kids who live in Mr. Pannell's district. The teen volunteers write letters, solicit donations, shop, wrap gifts and help coordinate the program."

I'm answering the phone and sorting the mail, sending off letters to certain people, faxing papers, filing notes and invitations after the councilman has looked at them—all kinds of stuff that I've never done before and wouldn't normally learn. It's a lot of fun.

—High school Senior Jaime Stokes,
Volunteer in the Office of a
Sacramento City Councilman

▼

You can't sound vague or uninformed when taking incoming calls.

The teen volunteers in the Sacramento city council office put in about 10 hours a week. Jones lets them spread the hours to fit whatever is convenient for their school schedule. One teen, for example, came in regularly every morning, from 8 to 10, five days a week. "She loved it," says Jones. "Most of them love it. The teens here now have morning classes and they're in the office from 2 to 5. If they have to be absent, I try to give them a break. Everybody gets sick, everybody needs days off."

Anybody can call up and say, "I'd like to volunteer with a city council person or the mayor" and we'd try to accommodate them.

—Nancy Gilder, Aide to the Mayor
of Denver, Colorado

In some cities and towns, the mayor shows a strong interest in having teen volunteers in the office. A good example is Phoenix, Arizona, where one of the mayor's aides, Paul Berumen, reports, "Our mayor is very committed to youth. Our program is just a formal expression of his commitment."

Berumen explains that while the teens gain valuable experience by working in the office, the staff members gain valuable and rewarding experience as well. "As a policymaker, you think you know what's going on, but sometimes the teens bring with them experiences that provide you a new and different perspective. Sometimes you have to ask them what they think. It is a rewarding experience to have them help in the office. We're trying to positively affect a young person's future. That's where I think we get the most out of it."

If you worked in the Phoenix mayor's office, your daily tasks would run the gamut from writing letters and getting out mail to handling phone calls from constituents and opening and sorting incoming mail. In addition to the general office work, you would have opportunities to attend various meetings. This would mean "shadowing" or accompanying Berumen or other executive team members to meetings, so you would get the feel of what's going on and how certain issues are handled.

Working in the mayor's office is an eye-opening experience. You get to see how city government works.
—Paul Berumen, Aide to the Mayor of Phoenix, Arizona

THE YOUTH COMMISSION

In many cities, a youth commission has been set up by the mayor's office or the city council. Teenagers are appointed to the commission, usually for terms of one or two years. They meet at least once a month and set the group's agenda on projects to be tackled over the course of several months or a year.

(Continued on page 25)

(Continued from page 24)

Recently, for example, the youth commission in Denver, Colorado, decided to make education issues its chief concern. During the campaign period before the November elections, it set up a debate among candidates for the board of education. In a public forum, members of the youth commission sat onstage facing the candidates and questioned them about their views on various policies set by the board. Then, after the election, those who had been elected to the board found even more focused questions coming to them from the youth commission.

"It was heavy stuff," says Nancy Gilder, an aide in the Denver mayor's office who works directly with the youth commission, "since we had just stopped busing."

In Phoenix, the mayor and the eight city council members each appoint one teenager to serve a two-year term on the mayor's youth and education commission, an official commission of the city. The nine-member group meets monthly. According to Paul Berumen, one of the mayor's aides, it gives the teens "direct input on city activities, overseeing a number of programs—from a partnership luncheon to specific initiatives regarding education. They get formal input into various programs and participate in them."

If you'd like to be appointed to your city's youth commission, send a letter to the mayor's office, describing your interest in being appointed. Or someone from the mayor's education office may check in at your high school to see who is interested in being a candidate.

"We hold a small interview, nothing very formal," says Berumen, "to let them know the demand—that they meet once a month on a certain day for so many hours, and that they must make that commitment. Then they are formally appointed to the commission."

(Courtesy: GPHC/Denver, CO)

Teen volunteers from Greater Park Hill Community Center perform a variety of duties for Happy Haynes, a member of the city council of Denver, Colorado. These three teens help by filing papers in the council's district office.

If you can bring computer skills into the office of a city council member, so much the better. "Most of the teens have been doing a lot of work on the computer," says Happy Haynes, a member of the city council of Denver, Colorado. "They're helping to set up my databases and all my constituent files."

But that's not all. Haynes says her teen volunteers "do a little bit of everything. I try to give them a pretty well-rounded work experience. We have a small office so I can offer them the experience that a person normally would have in a very small business, which means everybody does a little bit of everything."

In an office like this, you may help handle what seem like hundreds of calls a day from a lot of people—constituents, other city officials and so on. You quickly learn telephone etiquette, a skill that will come in handy wherever you work. And you find out how to fight the never-ending battle of filing, which all government offices must cope with.

HELPING STATE LEGISLATORS

The city or town where you live elects representatives to your state's two legislative bodies, probably known (depending on the state you live in) as the state "Senate" and the "Assembly" or "House of Representatives." Chances are that they represent several communities within a district. (Since representation is based on population, a single urban city or county that is thickly populated may include a number of districts; where the population is more spread out, a single district may include several small cities or towns.) Let's look at one such representative for an example of opportunities to volunteer in government.

In the Connecticut capital of Hartford, State Senator Jim Fleming represents 13 towns within a central Connecticut district. He himself started his career in government as a teenage volunteer, and in 18 years in the state legislature he has welcomed more than 100 teens who have worked as volunteers in his office.

Fleming explains that teen volunteers do everything except vote. "They act in the capacity of the legislator. They attend hearings, write press releases, attend meetings—often two or more meetings are scheduled at the same time. They also do research and help constituents. And if they're interested, they get out and do some campaigning," says Fleming.

The senator reports that teen volunteers in his office work on projects from simple things such as writing a press release—which, Fleming admits "isn't all that simple"—to setting up office hours in 13 different towns, which means calling each town hall and making confirmed dates.

The senator has a policy that when volunteers start he'll get them involved in something right away. He expects that they can handle it. If they have questions, they will ask him and if not, he gives them free rein.

—Doug Moore, Aide to Connecticut State Senator Jim Fleming

Volunteers can get quite involved. Fleming recalls one teen volunteer who showed a strong interest when Connecticut was in the process of adopting legalized gambling. The senator opposed the planned legislation, and the high school volunteer helped do much of the research on it, including making many calls to New Jersey, where legalized gambling was already established.

"A typical project," says Fleming, "runs anywhere from writing a letter, to helping out a constituent, to doing a research project on a bill that's before the legislature. One example would be the casino, but there have been others."

As another example, Fleming cites legislation that was passed by the U.S. Congress to create the Farmington Wild Scenic River area. Getting it through Congress took 10 years, and over that period teens in his office worked on it at various times and attended public hearings all over northwestern Connecticut and southwestern Massachusetts.

(Courtesy: State Senator Jim Fleming, Hartford, CT)

Teenagers who volunteer on the staff of Connecticut State Senator Jim Fleming (pictured above) may work on office projects or perform research concerning proposed legislation.

FROM WRITING LETTERS TO CHAUFFEURING

There's really no limitation to what you may do as a teen volunteer in Connecticut State Senator Jim Fleming's office.

You may work on a research project or write letters responding to constituents who write in. When the legislature is in session and the senator is busy in the capitol, you may be asked to attend meetings that he cannot get to. And he'll be depending on you to take good notes at such meetings. When the senator is present, you'll sit in on meetings that he may be having with constituents or with members from a state agency who may be coming in to present an issue.

When you volunteer in an office such as Fleming's, you may also make trips around the voting district. This can mean spending all day Saturday with your senator or representative as he or she holds office hours in various town halls or other places. It can last into the evening as you "work" fund-raising events in advance of election day. Your duties may include acting as chauffeur, driving the representative to such events.

Doug Moore, an executive aide to Fleming, says the teenagers typically arrange their schedules so they come into the office one or two days a week. "They can arrange their classes so we get them from 12 o'clock on," he notes, "so we get a half day's work out of them. Obviously, their school-work comes first."

HELPING U.S. SENATORS AND MEMBERS OF CONGRESS

If you volunteer to work in the home office of a U.S. senator or a member of the House of Representatives, you will find the work quite similar to that in the offices of state legislators. But working for a member of the U.S. Congress usually puts a bigger feather in your cap.

During July and August 1997, several teen volunteers worked all day for two or three days a week in the home office of U.S. Congressman James H. Maloney, who represented Connecticut's Fifth Congressional District. Maloney's aide, Frieda Lucarelli, says, "They did almost everything. They were answering phones, making copies of letters, documents and newspaper clippings and going to events with the congressman."

People call their public officials for all kinds of reasons.

Typical duties in Maloney's office include responding to a broad range of requests from constituents. One of the things you learn in an office like this is that people call their public officials for all kinds of reasons, from getting prescriptions filled when they've run out, to how to get a seat belt removed from a car, to how to get commercial vehicles off a parkway that is supposed to be reserved for passenger cars.

Many such requests are beyond the control of the official or the office staff. "We have to pass them on to other agencies," says Lucarelli, "and that requires a letter saying here's what we've found out about this, or here's what you should do. The teens learn how to write those letters." For example, Lucarelli explains that the teens sent the complaint about commercial vehicles on the parkway to the right department in the state government.

Lucarelli helps the teen volunteers learn to handle all kinds of demands and requests. "Each one has to show that they can do it," she says, "step by step. We'll have them do an initial intake, and then go over the case and make a plan, even if it's very small, about what we're going to do with it. And then, depending on how complicated it is, they can sometimes carry that out and actually serve as the contact for the person."

"MAKING ADJUSTMENTS AND DEALS"

In the summer of 1997, before her senior year in high school, Melissa Colangelo volunteered in the office of U.S. Congresswoman Rosa L. DeLauro in New Haven, Connecticut. She worked there five days a week from 12:30 until 5: "We dealt with the congresswoman's constituents in the New Haven office, while her office in Washington handled the legislative issues."

Melissa found that each of DeLauro's caseworkers had jurisdiction over a certain set of issues. The caseworker she worked for dealt with the Post Office, the Federal Communications Commission, housing, utilities and requests for information. Melissa had to handle a number of issues and situations.

On certain days of the week Melissa took care of "call intake" on the telephone. "That meant I answered the phone and wrote down the name of whoever called," she explains, "and their issues, their concerns. Sometimes it was a legislative concern, asking the congresswoman to support certain bills. But most of the time it was a constituent calling with a

(Continued on page 33)

(Continued from page 32)

problem—someone was being evicted from their home or was having a problem because the postal service moved the box where they always deposited their mail, or they were having a problem with some sort of utility.

"We'd take down the information and from there we'd call the corporations that could help, or call the utility, and we'd negotiate." Melissa learned that much of the work was "a back-and-forth process between the constituent and the company involved in the problem." She spent her time writing letters, making phone calls "and making adjustments and deals."

Because one of her areas of specialization was housing, she had to make many calls to city housing authorities and to the Department of Housing and Urban Development. "A lot of it was negotiation," she says, "and it was incredibly interesting."

U.S. senators do not represent districts. Each state's two senators represent their entire states. In states that are geographically large, you can probably find more than one local office of a senator. New York's Senator Daniel Patrick Moynihan, for example, maintains offices not only in Washington and New York City but also in Buffalo, at the western end of the state, and in Oneonta, in the central part of the state. So you can often find opportunities to volunteer for a senator even if you do not live near the state capital or the senator's hometown.

Let's compare the work for teen volunteers in two distinctive offices—the Washington office of Senator Moynihan and the home office, in Hartford, of Connecticut's Senator Joseph L. Lieberman.

"High school students volunteer as interns for us throughout the year while they are in school as well as in the summer," says Heather Ackerman, an aide to Senator Moynihan. "Some may get credits toward graduation, and maybe have to write a paper on their experience or keep a weekly journal on what they do in the office."

The high school students usually come in one day a week. Ackerman says they are treated the same as college students who come into the office on a semester-long program, and they do the same things as the college students do.

The teen duties are—"first and foremost," as she puts it—to help out in the mailroom. "That's the heart of our correspondence operation," she says. "That includes opening the mail, sorting and stamping it in and preparing it for the permanent staff to read, monitor and sort according to issue."

Beyond handling the large volume of mail, the teen volunteers take on a wide range of tasks, from photocopying to sitting in for one of the legislative assistants at a hearing.

"What really happens here," says Ackerman, "is that they have to prove themselves. If a staff member gives an intern a photocopying job, for example, and they get it back and it's unsatisfactory or completely wrong, then obviously they're not going to say, 'Go sit in on this hearing for me.'

"For the most part," Ackerman says, "the teens' day involves handling a lot of the mail, doing copying and running many errands, like picking up things at the Library of Congress or over at the Senate Library."

Suppose you are volunteering in that office and a research assistant needs to write a memo to his or her legislative assistant. You might be asked to assist by doing some research in the Congressional Research Service or in the Library of Congress—wherever

(Courtesy: Senator Joe L. Lieberman, Washington, DC)

Heather Picazio (far right) began as a teenage volunteer for Senator Joe L. Lieberman (left), who represents Connecticut in Washington, D.C. Posing with them is Mathew Cohen, an intern working in the senator's office.

that research may take you. "The teen volunteers," says Ackerman, "really provide support to the entire legislative and administrative staffs."

Now compare the experiences of Heather Picazio, an aide in the
Hartford office of Senator Lieberman, who represents Connecticut
in Washington. Here, teen volunteers work under a different system
of management. "Generally," says Picazio, "they are assigned a
mentor in the office, either a caseworker or state director."

Under the mentor's direction, the teens help out with scheduling
and other assignments—from clipping newspapers to filing, from
answering the phones to researching information for constituents
who call the office. The typical questions range from future bills
that may be coming up, to when legislation is expected to be voted
on in the Senate, to how the senator voted on particular issues.
"It's just tons of different things," says Picazio.

When the senator is in the state, the teen volunteers have an
opportunity to sit in on meetings and to go to other events the
senator is attending. "And, of course," adds Picazio, "they can get
their photos taken, at the end of the summer, with the senator and
he signs the picture and all that kind of stuff. It's a neat thing."

A CAPITAL IDEA

If you live in or near the capital city of your state, you may be able
to volunteer not only in the offices of members of the legislature,
but also in the offices of the lieutenant governor or the governor.
In California, over several years, the lieutenant governor's office in
Sacramento has put some 50 high school students to work as
unpaid interns. By arrangement with their schools, they get academic credit. "A lot of times," says Trish Fontana, assistant to Lieutenant Governor Gray Davis of California, "these are juniors and
graduating seniors who have completed the requirements for col-

lege, so they're looking to fill their afternoons. The teen volunteers can work on anything in the office that they would like to pursue.

"I expose them to everything," says Fontana, "and then sometimes I find that they're geared more toward the research and the analytical."

Here, as in the other government offices you have already read about, correspondence with constituents is one of the basic tasks. Letters arrive in batches of dozens, hundreds, sometimes thousands. "They can be on any topic," says Fontana, "and I try to gauge the high school students' interest toward handling them."

The teens also help assemble press packets and put out press releases. "Some love working with the press and watching an issue go through a press conference," says Fontana, "and then doing the follow-up on that. They do some of the simple filing, some of the phone answering. My philosophy is that if you're at your desk every day, you're not learning. I push them to go watch hearings and legislative sessions. They go to anything that's happening in this building that they're interested in or they can learn a lot from."

I have them pick a couple of pieces of legislation to follow and track and then write a brief report on. So I make sure they're paying attention on the slow days in the building.

**—Trish Fontana, Aide to
the Lieutenant Governor of California**

Fontana speaks of a particular student whom she found "amazing." The student worked 40 hours a week during the summer before her junior year in high school. She spent most of her time developing a policy binder, or briefing paper, for the lieutenant governor. "That is something," says Fontana, "that usually a high school student isn't well-rounded and exposed enough to be able to do. She immersed herself. She is just one of the most outstanding young people I've ever worked with."

What kind of hours might you be expected to put in if you volunteer in a lieutenant governor's office? During the school year, says Fontana, she would expect you to spend 10 to 12 hours a week. "I normally encourage them not to come in every day for two hours," she says, "because they just don't get the impact that way. They sometimes walk in on a very hectic day, and they don't get the flavor during that short a time. I encourage them to come for three to four hours three times a week. Sometimes when they don't have school, or during their holiday breaks, they'll come in at a different time, without being asked, to see what goes on during a different time of the day. They'll say, 'Hey, Trish, can I come in the mornings?' I'm very flexible with their schedules. We work them in at all different times of the day."

The summer brings teens whom Fontana calls "the real die-hard volunteers." They work without getting any academic credit, she notes. "They're just doing this," she observes, "for pure experience. Sometimes they'll put in two full days even though they have another summer job. They can't work here on weekends, so they'll take two days off the summer job during the week and work here on those days."

TWO TEEN VOLUNTEERS DESCRIBE THEIR WORK

At the office of the lieutenant governor of California, we talked to Lela Young and Brian Wise. They volunteered here over the summer of 1997, after Lela had completed 10th grade and Brian had graduated from high school.

Q. On a day-to-day basis, what kind of work did you do?

A. LELA: Basically, it depends on the day. When I started out, when I was first learning how to do things, I did some filing and corresponding with constituent mail. I learned a lot of general office procedures, such as how to answer the phones at the front desk.

A. BRIAN: To begin with, I had to respond to constituent mail. We did administrative kinds of things—the various duties of running the office, setting up appointments and so on.

Q. Then did your responsibilities increase?

A. LELA: Yes, after my first couple of weeks, as I got more comfortable, they got a feel for what I could do and started giving me bigger assignments. And at the time they were putting together research on some of the ethnic groups in California, especially the Latino community and the Asian–Pacific Islanders. The project was really interesting. I pulled up different kinds of information on that and condensed it into a final paper.

A. BRIAN: Trish Fontana initiated a new program and handed the duties over to me—she put me in charge of it. It involved setting up the e-mail system. Because we're advancing into the 21st century, electronic mail has become the new way of communicating. We set up a system whereby the lieutenant governor can actually receive constituent e-mail and respond to it within 24 hours. Mail received by the postal service can sometimes take three to five weeks to go through the reply process. E-mail gets a response to a constituent a whole lot faster.

Q. So you both became responsible for original work— not just "make-work" projects?

A. LELA: Yes. They would tell us to dig up something on a given subject and we had to go find it. For these things in particular, we were looking for the lieutenant governor's history with the various groups—

(Courtesy: Gray Davis, Lieutenant Governor, State of California)

Posing with Gray Davis, the lieutenant governor of California, are teenage volunteers Lela Young, Courtney Holst, (center), Deborah Slon, Joseph Schultz, Michelle Loera and Brian Wise.

what he had done, what he had been involved with, and also his position on current legislation. I learned how to use a program on the computer so I could find out about the different bills that had been put through recently. Then I'd look up general information, such as some of the census reports and other things like that. The office staff members were really nice and they helped me when I needed assistance.

A. BRIAN: Yes, I set up the e-mail system so we can provide the fastest service to the constituent—because that's who the lieutenant governor works for.

Q. What other projects have you worked on?

A. **LELA:** I also put together a book on the history of women in California. The office had put together a little book on the subject, but they wanted to do a more finished version. I helped go through and make changes and additions to it. That was interesting.

A. **BRIAN:** While I was there we were organizing the policy handbook. We set it up so the lieutenant governor could be more informed on the entire state. It gives him facts and figures pertaining to the different constituencies that he has.

I could be in the middle of a project and someone would need something that day. I would stop what I was doing to help them. They might want me to do research or run to different offices and pick up things or hand something out. It was always really interesting.
—**Lela Young, 10th-grade Volunteer in the Office of the Lieutenant Governor of California**

WORKING FOR A PRESS SECRETARY

Michelle Lee, who is press secretary to the secretary of state in California, got her start in government work as a teen volunteer. "Sometimes in high school," she says, "you kind of know what you want to do in advance because of the pressure of applying to college. Government was something I was always interested in, and my volunteering really reinforced that. It enhanced my interest in the dynamics of government."

(Continued on page 42)

(Continued from page 41)

What would you be doing if you were a volunteer in Lee's office? Since the office is responsible for releasing any news pertaining to the secretary of state, you would frequently find yourself helping to get out press releases to the California capitol press corps, making some 95 copies of press releases and assembling that many press kits when needed.

But that's not all you would do. "I like volunteers to help with press calls," Lee says. "My unit's main job is to help the media. Sometimes a reporter will call and say, 'What was the voter turnout for the 1992 primary in California, or in this county?' And we have reference material here that answers such questions. It's not that the teenagers will act as spokespersons but they can help with this kind of reference work. I like to elevate them to that level. That's one of the objectives that we have for the interns here."

If you volunteer in this kind of office, one of your greatest responsibilities is maintaining the filing system on the countless issues that concern the secretary of state, from voting to campaign financing. You will help to obtain needed documents from other divisions or departments of the government. Many documents are not readily accessible on the computer. They have to be copied manually from sources or files that date back to precomputer days.

The secretary of state is usually responsible for the registry of corporations and the records of notaries public. "It's just a very wide array of registration information," says Lee, "so we

(Continued on page 43)

(Courtesy: Bill Jones, Secretary of State, Sacramento, CA)

Michelle Lee (left) began as a volunteer with the teen program for the secretary of state's office in California a few years ago and now works there full time as a press assistant. Also on staff are Deputy Communications Director Alfie Charles (center) and the Secretary of State's Press Secretary Shirley Washington (right).

have a pretty large amount of material that we are concerned with and write about, and the volunteers are primarily responsible for keeping the files."

Because she is a veteran of the teen program—"I wasn't there too long ago," says Lee—she understands what might be interesting to the volunteers. "I try to keep them exposed to what's really going on not only in the news but around our

(Continued on page 44)

43

(Continued from page 43)

government and our working environment here," she says. "We try to keep a very open line of communication and we're very team oriented. So they can get a sense of working in an office team environment and learning organizational skills.

"Lots of times we'll be working on our everyday tasks and something will come up in the news, like for instance the term-limits lawsuit, or the court will come up with something, and we'll need to drop everything and publish something to the media—maybe our comment or how we're affected by whatever happened—and then pick up on our tasks later. So it's a good way of learning how to organize and prioritize work."

HELPING WITH REGISTRATION AND TURNOUT

Suppose you don't want to volunteer in the office of an elected official in government but you do have an interest in how government works and in the democratic electoral process. You can help broaden public understanding of the process and interest in voting by working with various organizations.

Probably the best known is the League of Women Voters (LWV). One of the first things you should know about this organization, which has local chapters or affiliates in cities and towns across America, is that—despite its name—men are welcome to be members. The second thing you should know is that, despite the fact that you cannot vote until you are 18 years old, you can be an active participant in LWV activities when you are younger.

For example, look at the League of Young Women Voters of Weston High School in Connecticut. (Note that they add the word "young" to their title.) It includes high school students who have shown an interest in the issues during recent elections, but who do not want to get into the nitty-gritty of partisan politics.

Margaret Wirtenberg, president of the town's LWV, explains that one of the organization's tasks is to work at debates held during election campaigns. "LWV members ferry the questions from the audience to our speakers," she says. "And they have some questions of their own, too, which the speakers are asked. They are very serious."

Wirtenberg notes that the young LWV members were so encouraged by this work that they cosponsored—with the adult LWV—a breakfast for their state senator and a number of representatives before the legislative session began. The teen members sat with the adult members at each table and participated in questioning the legislators.

Next, the League of Young Women Voters joined the LWV in cosponsoring a "party to celebrate democracy," at which they asked three members of the town's board of selectmen to address the question of their vision for the town in the 21st century.

"Our high school teens are very interested and certainly motivated," says Wirtenberg. "They're talking about becoming educated about issues so they can become responsible voters. They even drew up a charter to register the group with the high school. It's a great privilege to work with them. I respect them tremendously."

WEBSITE FOR THE LWV

If you know how to design websites, you may be able to do the kind of volunteer job that two ninth-grade boys did for the LWV of West Hartford, Connecticut. They designed the LWV's web page and presented it to the league's board of directors. After the board approved the design, the boys completed the technical work to put it on-line.

"They had to meet the standards of the LWV, which, of course, is a national organization," says the West Hartford organization's president, Becky Swanson-Bowers, "and put information out there that the league considered pertinent."

The teens also came up with ideas. For example, they created a section on where to vote. From the registrar of voters, they obtained a map showing all the assembly districts in the area, as well as all the polling districts. They put that map into the computer. They color-coded it so that anyone visiting the website could find out where to go to vote. If you visit the site, for example, and click onto the map of the area, you can then click onto the color of the assembly district where you live. The street addresses are there, so that if you don't know your district ahead of time, you can figure it out from the map.

And when you go to the next page, to find your polling district, you pull up another map, with smaller areas. Clicking onto your polling district gives you not only the address of your polling place but also a picture of the particular building that is your polling place in the district, so you know exactly what to look for.

The ninth-graders did more. They put in a link that enables users to type in their home addresses and the addresses of polling places. The website then comes up with written directions as well as a map showing how to go directly from the voter's home to the polling place.

In a "first" in their state, the LWV obtained permission from the office of the secretary of state to put the voter registration form on the website. "You can print it out and mail it in to the registrar in your town," says Swanson-Bowers. "And there's a list on the web page of all the registrars of voters in the towns in the greater area. It also provides lists of who the elected officials are, as well as information about the league and its history, who the league's officers are, what our calendar of events is, and how to join our league.

"The teens also set it up so you can e-mail an official, your senator, for example, directly from the site. They did all that, as volunteers, over a period of about nine months."

Because the LWV is nationwide, you may be able to do a job like this wherever you are—if you have the computer know-how and a forward-thinking LWV organization in your community.

VOTER REGISTRATION: A GRASSROOTS EFFORT

First getting people to register so they are able to vote and then getting them to go out and vote on election day are two great challenges that our democracy faces. In many communities, you will find continuing efforts being made to get citizens to understand the value of registering and voting.

As an example, let's look at the Southwest Voter Registration Project (SVREP). Headquartered in San Antonio, Texas, it works in 13 states of the Southwest and West to organize coalitions determined to register minority voters. SVREP welcomes high-school-age volunteers. San Antonio Project Coordinator Johnnie Rodriguez talks about the program:

> Our high school student volunteers go out with me to target precincts in the surrounding area to help build up the number of voters in the precinct. They not only register the people to vote, they also get out the vote on election day. We get them involved in doing house meetings that provide voter education on the issues. We bring in speakers and get our teens involved in helping organize these events. They help decide on the agenda and put it together, for example.

Rodriguez says this grassroots effort focuses strictly on the neighborhoods and stores, trying to get large numbers of eligible voters to register, especially before an election year.

(Courtesy: Johnnie Rodriguez/SVREP, San Antonio, TX)

Working for the Southwest Voter Registration Project (SVREP) enables teen volunteers to get feedback on community concerns. Tim Duda, pictured above, is a student adviser at South San Antonio High School in Texas and helps Johnnie Rodriguez, SVREP coordinator, with scheduling volunteers. In this photo, Duda is being interviewed at the high school.

"We keep track of how many people are registered in the precinct," he says, "and how many we can get to commit to vote. We have a pledge card that says, 'Yes, I will pledge to vote on election day,' and that's a source of contact as well. We create our database out of that and we also do a phone bank."

Rodriguez reports that the teen volunteers participate in all of that. "They do the phone bank and also help organize the house meetings," he says. "The high school students do a lot of the block-walking stuff. They're in touch and they're eager to learn, so it's easy to break them into the grassroots efforts. It's a learning process for them because they get to hear the concerns of the people in the community, and they get excited. The feedback from the community just builds pictures in their minds as to what really is out there. I guess they get a sense of what the real world is about."

What else can you do as a volunteer in government and politics? If you have a driver's license, you can help take voters to the polls on election day if they don't have transportation. If you want to be nonpartisan about it, you can divide your driving time between the two major political parties. Election day, however, comes probably only once a year.

If you want to be partisan, you can help campaign for the candidates—and the party—of your choice. That can get you into phoning, stuffing envelopes, filing, chauffeuring, even public speaking. And it can occupy all the time you are willing to give it for several weeks, if not months, before the election.

CHAPTER THREE

What It Takes to Volunteer in Government

*P*articipating in government will provide you with challenging and rewarding experiences. As a teen volunteer, there are several items that will be required of you. These include:

- Strength and stamina,
- Use of a car,
- Commitment and attitude,
- Basic skills,
- Attitude and interest.

You need a high level of energy.

STRENGTH AND STAMINA

You need to be in good physical condition to work in this area. You need a high level of energy. There may be times when you will put in some long hours. Good powers of concentration and the ability to pay attention to details will be helpful, too.

USE OF A CAR

How old do you have to be? That depends. Many volunteer opportunities are open to any high school student in any grade, but often the opportunity depends on your having a way to get to it. If you are under driving age, that means you depend on someone else to get you there and take you home again. If you have your operator's permit and the use of a car, the opportunity is wide open.

A lot depends on their transportation ability—their ability to get here. We look for juniors and seniors because most of them drive.

—Paul Berumen, aide to the Mayor of Phoenix, Arizona

"I TRY TO GIVE THEM A BREAK"

"Usually I take whoever comes," says Denver City Council-woman Happy Haynes, "but I interview them and make them jump through the hoops. I ask them, 'What do you want? Why do you want this job? What kind of skills do you have?'

"Most of our kids have been referred through a neighborhood organization here that offers a summer youth program. The kids apply through them and then the organization refers the youngsters to me. The organization selects a couple of applicants that they think are pretty sharp, but I always try to interview them. I've never turned anyone away."

Haynes says she once had "a couple of boys whose skills were extremely weak. It was obvious that they weren't accustomed to doing chores—like throwing out the trash. So I kept them on task, kept them focused on doing work and understanding why work skills are necessary. It was difficult, but I stuck with them all summer long, and they improved by the end.

(Continued on page 52)

(Continued from page 51)

"The other kids I've had have been just extraordinary. And they usually are in the 13-, 14- and 15-year-old range. Part of the reason I take this age group is because the older kids can go get jobs and these kids can't. I try to give them a break and give them a real work experience that they usually wouldn't be able to get at that age."

COMMITMENT

As in any work you volunteer for, you can be sure the professionals you work with will expect dependability more than anything else. They don't want to spend their time training you if they cannot rely on you to be there when you said you'd be there and do what you said you'd do.

I've found that interns who really like it make the time to come down. They get a lot out of it if they put a lot into it. Others come down and try it for a week and see what it's like and that's enough for them.
— **Connecticut State Senator Jim Fleming**

What makes you dependable is your own interest in the work. Do you have a strong interest in government and politics? Would you like to teach these subjects someday? Are you a politician your-self—active in student government, the student council, the debating club? Does the field of journalism and reporting the facts of

(Courtesy: GPHC/Denver, CO)

Happy Haynes uses many volunteers from the Greater Park Hill Community Center of Denver, Colorado. These girls worked with the 1995 youth program helping to clean up a Denver neighborhood for senior citizens.

public life appeal to you? Your interest in one or more of these areas will dictate your commitment to helping to make our democratic government, at all levels, work well—and to increasing public understanding of how it works.

We're pretty excited when someone in their early or mid-teens shows an interest in government and in volunteering.
—Heather Ackerman, Aide to
Senator Daniel Patrick Moynihan of New York

BASIC SKILLS

The most valuable skills you can bring to volunteer work in government and politics are "people skills"—the ability to get along with others and work cooperatively on a team. You do not necessarily need to have specific office skills, such as touch typing, data management and filing. You can learn a particular office's filing system on the job, as well as how to operate copying machines and telephone switchboards or panels. In some offices, you can find staff people who are willing to help you learn computer skills. But you start with an advantage if you already know how to operate basic office equipment.

Two important things that government offices look for are good schoolwork and basic writing skills. "We want to make sure that they are doing well in school," says Heather Picazio, aide to U.S. Senator Joseph L. Lieberman of Connecticut. "We have them send in a writing sample. They need to write letters and we need to know that they can handle that task efficiently. We have their transcripts sent here, so we can make sure they are good students and will be conscientious about coming into the office. There's a lot of different things that we look at."

You should have some decent writing skills—that's the first thing you need.
        —Jordan Paul, High School Senior Volunteer,
    Office of Connecticut State Senator Jim Fleming

If you are being considered for a volunteer spot in any government office, don't hesitate to tell whoever interviews you about any experience you have had in government or politics. Have you been elected a class officer? Served on your school's student council? Belonged to a club in which you were elected to a responsible position? Captained a team? Represented your class or your school in any citywide, statewide, or national conferences?

If you are thinking about a career in law or journalism, make that known, too. Public speaking in your school's debating society, appearances on stage with the drama club, reporting news or writing a column in the school paper—all are good qualifications for those wanting to volunteer at a government office. They indicate you know something about thinking on your feet and communicating with others.

WRITE A FACT SHEET ABOUT YOURSELF

"My philosophy," says Trish Fontana, aide to the lieutenant governor of California, "is that you can't expect teens to be prepared as if they were doing this for a job interview. You can't ask about what skills they have and what qualifies them. Instead of a résumé, I have them write a fact sheet about themselves that lists the classes they've taken, hobbies, jobs

(Continued on page 56)

(Continued from page 55)

that they've worked on. I try not to have them feel that they're getting the 10 questions and they have to answer them right or they're not going to be accepted. I sit down and basically have a conversation with them, chat with them, try to get them to open up a little bit.

"I interview 18 students per semester, after they've been through an initial screening process. And I take two or three of them. If they have computer skills, that's wonderful. If they don't, we'll train them. They go through an orientation the first week. Basically, my philosophy is, anybody can come in and do it."

ATTITUDE AND INTEREST

In any government office, you will be expected to show a positive attitude toward the work. That means you cannot be shy about tackling any particular assignment or about dealing with people, whether they are staff people in the office or the public (that is, the constituents of the officeholder) that come in or write or call.

Working among us all, the kids get a really good experience here. Not only that, but I find that it enriches us.
                                    —Happy Haynes, City Councilwoman,
                                                Denver, Colorado

It takes a certain amount of self-discipline to volunteer in a busy government office. In the office of any member of a city council or other legislative body, you may find yourself asked to do work that may seem meaningless to you. Why, for instance, must you spend so much time on a boring job like clipping marked-up newspapers from towns all over the map? The answer is that those clippings help the elected official to keep up to date on what is happening in all the areas he or she represents. They let the official know what people talk and care about. So it's important not to become frustrated by such an assignment.

Be aware that you will experience every aspect of the total system. You will be immersed. But don't get carried away by your own importance. As Heather Picazio, aide to Senator Lieberman, puts it, "Don't come in here expecting to write new economic policy for the senator to start reading."

Don't get carried away by your own importance.

Connecticut State Senator Jim Fleming, who has welcomed many teen volunteers in his office, says, "We used to do a formal application process. But what we've found is that word of mouth works at the high schools. Whenever I go out and speak to a group, I always say, 'If you're interested in coming down to the capitol, give me a call.' And I try to say yes to whoever would like to come down. They have to be capable of reading and writing and so forth. All of them are. And they need to provide their own transportation. Some of them can spend a day or two and some can spend the whole session. It just depends on what their schedule will allow. So as long as they have permission from their parents and from the school, we like to have as many as we can have down there."

Fleming adds that he also uses volunteer interns from colleges in the Hartford, Connecticut, area, but that he finds that his high school volunteers "certainly are the same caliber as college students. And they're from all the 13 different towns in my district."

How much do the teen volunteers contribute to the senator's office? Doug Moore, executive aide to Fleming, can answer that. "This place could not operate without interns," he says. "When we're in session, the amount of mail, the amount of constituent calls that come in, if the paid staff alone were to handle it we'd get piled up. We have interns that come in here and volunteer their time, and boy, is it appreciated!"

INDEPENDENCE AND OBJECTIVITY

There is something else that it takes to volunteer in certain situations. You must hold onto your independence and objectivity. The problem? Let Johnnie Rodriguez, San Antonio Project Coordinator for the Southwest Voter Registration Project (SVREP), describe it. "One thing bad that everybody is already catching on to," he says, "is what we call 'bounty hunting.' It's the politicians during the election year hiring students to go do the block-walking for them. They pay them."

Rodriguez points out that an organization like SVREP has a hard time getting funding and cannot afford to pay its volunteers. "I feel that you have to give something back to the community," he says, "and when they pay students off for block-walking, it takes away because now the teens say, 'Why should we go out there and walk for nothing when the politicians are going to pay us?' A lot of them did that this past election, and they got a taste of it, but that's the wrong message to send to the students."

EVERYTHING CONNECTS

Brian Wise, who took advantage of an opportunity to volunteer in the office of the lieutenant governor of California just after he graduated from high school, had been active in student government during his high school years in a small California town some 150 miles from Sacramento. "Ever since I was very

(Continued on page 59)

(Continued from page 58)

little," says Brian, "I've been very community-service oriented. My family brought me up to appreciate the government, and that's where my career thoughts lie as I go into college."

Brian expects to major in government journalism, with a minor in business administration. He has his sights set on law school after that, and hopes to attend Harvard Law. Describing his path in this direction, he says, "I've really seen what government can do for people as well as to people. And I've always looked to government and civil service as a way of fulfilling my civic duty. I feel that I have a place in government as a career."

One of Brian's favorite experiences was his trip to Washington, D.C., as a delegate to the Presidential Classroom. "That's a conference set up around the federal government," he says. "It takes 50 students for a week—altogether, about 300 students over six weeks. We got a look behind the scenes of government. We held debates on the floor of the Senate and the House of Representatives, and we had meetings with our legislators—things like that." What led to Brian's summer as a volunteer in Sacramento? He had volunteered in the offices of members of his town's city council, where his leadership abilities were recognized.

"That was one of the best experiences," he says, "because not only did I get to meet people around the city but I got to meet people around the state." Eventually, a visit by the California secretary of state led to work as a summer volunteer in the office of the lieutenant governor.

"Everything worked out for me," says Brian. "Government comes down to the smallest city, the smallest town, the smallest little urban development. Everything connects and everybody's important."

What's in It for You?

*O*ne question everybody asks about volunteering is, "What's in it for me?" There are a number of answers to that question.

CAREER AND COLLEGE BENEFITS

Volunteering in government and politics can help lead to a career in this field. It gives you hands-on experience that can help you decide whether this is the kind of area you want to major in during college or go to work in after college. There's nothing better than finding out what goes on in any particular kind of work before you invest a lot of study time and career time in it. As Heather Picazio, aide to U.S. Senator Joseph L. Lieberman from Connecticut, puts it, "It gives you a taste of 'Gee, would I like to do this, would I not like to do this?' I volunteered here, and I loved it. I ended up working here. So you never know."

I like to have the teens exposed to everything in the building, and maybe it will help them decide on a career path or what they want to do or don't want to do. I started as a volunteer 12 years ago not knowing what I wanted to do or where I wanted to go. The opportunity was there, and I'm just so grateful.

**—Trish Fontana, Aide to
the Lieutenant Governor of California**

(Courtesy: Congressman Sam Gedjenson, Bozrah, CT)

Working as a teenage volunteer in government helps you gain hands-on experience working with the public. Congressman Sam Gejdenson (center) represents Connecticut in Washington, D.C., and took time out during his campaign to pose with some of his teenage volunteers in Bozrah, Connecticut.

No one knows just how many teenage volunteers in government wind up later on as staff aides to elected officials or as successful politicians. Doug Moore, aide to Connecticut State Senator Jim Fleming, was a volunteer intern himself. So was Fleming, who headed Teenage Young Republicans of Simsbury (TAYRS), Connecticut, when he was in high school and at that time also volunteered in the office of his state representative. After college, Fleming won a seat in Connecticut's General Assembly. Over some 18 years he moved up to the state senate and ultimately achieved the position of senate majority leader.

"I wouldn't be surprised," says Moore, "to find that as many as 30 percent of the current General Assembly, which has 187 members, had been volunteer interns themselves. The number is unbelievable. And a lot of the staff people who work in the capital are here because they interned at one time or another."

"FIRSTHAND EXPERIENCE OF THE GOOD AND THE BAD"

"Some of the volunteers have become very involved in the political side of it," says Connecticut State Senator Jim Fleming.

"I've always said to them, it's not a requirement but if you are interested in getting involved politically, if you want to see what that side of it is like, let me know. We run for election every two years, and very often the interns have become involved in actually working on the campaigns as well. Setting up fund-raisers, scheduling and going out and shaking people's hands—the nuts and bolts of grassroots politics—give you real firsthand experience of the good and the bad that goes on. You see everything. You see the tough votes and the easy votes. So if you're interested in politics, you learn what it's really like."

Fleming points out that high school students are not nearly as sure as college students about what they want to do in life. "I

(Continued on page 63)

(Continued from page 62)

think in a couple of instances," he says, "volunteering as a teenager has given them an interest in attending a particular college and taking a certain course of study and then coming back to town or to the district and becoming involved politically. The best example I can give you of that would be one of my interns who ended up becoming a state legislator after having spent a semester with me. So they do get a lot out of it."

By the time you complete a semester or two, or a summer, volunteering in a government office, you should be able to put together a résumé or brief written record of your experience and what you gained from it. This can range from specific working skills to a broader understanding of what makes people tick. This will be valuable when you go to any job or college interview, for it will help the person interviewing you to see just what you have to offer.

In fact, you can use your experience as a good basis for the essay that will probably be required on your college application. That's what Jordan Paul did after he volunteered in the office of Connecticut State Senator Jim Fleming during his senior year in high school. "I talked about how teenagers are sometimes plagued by cynicism," he says, "but I made the point that when you do something like this, you see how government and the system really do work. There are people here who make it work and work hard for a lot of other people, their fellow citizens. Maybe it sounds kind of corny, but it gives you a new faith."

I learned what it is like to work in an office—a real work-place. If you just do it for a weekend, you don't get a real feel for being there. I was there for six weeks and I was included in what was going on. I would attend staff meetings, staff luncheons and dinners. I felt that they cared about my opinions. The best way to learn about all this is to put yourself into the situation and see whether you like it.

—Lela Young, 10th-grade Volunteer in
the Office of Lieutenant Governor Gray Davis
of California

THE DISCIPLINE

One of the many benefits you get from this kind of volunteering is working on various projects with adults in genuine work situations. You learn to deal with real-life conditions—with meeting people's specific needs. In effect, in any government office, the public is your client.

Vincene Jones, aide to a Sacramento, California, city councilman, describes the job discipline you can expect to find. "They learn," she says, "how to go out into the world to work. Whether or not they want to make this particular type of job their own, it gives them the responsibility and shows them the different requirements. For an example, they find out they can't wear baggy jeans everywhere. You have to dress a certain way. We do have a dress code in this office."

Jones makes the point that whether you are going on to college or to a full-time job, the experience gives you life skills—being on time, calling in when you're going to be late, calling in when you must be absent, making up the time you have missed. "I look at all that," she says, "as life skills."

You also gain specific work skills, from the etiquette of answering phones to how to make concise and understandable notes on incoming calls, from the precise discipline of filing systems (you will seldom encounter a headache bigger than trying to retrieve something that is "lost" in the files) to coping with the need to revise a busy official's appointments schedule frequently.

I observe how well the teen volunteers are doing with basic skills, like language, filing and writing notes. I try to give them guidance about areas they should work on, always stressing, "Do you see why this is important?"
—**Happy Haynes, Denver, Colorado, City Councilwoman**

THE REAL WORLD OUT THERE

What's in it for you when you volunteer in any government office is a good, practical introduction to the world beyond the classroom. You can read about government and serving the public. You can listen to your teachers and guidance counselors. But until you spend time in a hands-on situation, like some of those described here, you will not gain the special insights these typical teen volunteers have.

Jordan Paul, high school senior volunteer in the office of Connecticut State Senator Jim Fleming, sees that. "It's one of the best things I've done in school," he says. "I know it's outside of school, but it has added an entirely different dimension to the learning process. Seeing how something really functions and reading about it in a book are entirely different."

In his work in the state senator's office, Jordan sees facets of how the government works that give him "a different take on it than you read in the newspaper. All you hear is cynicism about government, and you see these people here in session and it's a really incredible experience. You see all these people working for the state, working for something bigger than themselves. You learn about the intricacies and all the responsibilities they have, and you really live it. To me it is truly amazing."

(Courtesy: Nicole Puente/SVREP, San Antonio, TX)

During your classes at school, you may study about government and visualize how you can serve the public. But actually participating is a totally different matter. Sonja Sosa gets some real-world experience as a teen volunteer with the Southwest Voter Registration Project by walking house-to-house registering voters.

Jordan's state senator, Jim Fleming, sees something else that's in it for the teen volunteer. He takes the teens along on many of his frequent tours of the district he represents. Those tours, he points out, "expose them to everything that we have to deal with in society." Included are some of the state's wealthiest neighborhoods and some of its poorest, the interiors of its overpopulated prisons and of its crowded gambling casinos. The teens even accompany him when he joins the police for regular patrols.

If you're interested in government or in becoming involved even as a social worker, a volunteer internship with the legislature is a good one—because you'll get to see so much.
—Jim Fleming, Connecticut State Senator

Sometimes you get your practical experience—and the opportunity to prove you can handle it—in strong doses. Denver City Councilwoman Happy Haynes says she often subjects her teen volunteers to "trial by fire." They find themselves under heavy pressure to go right to work and make a contribution. "I don't think I've had one over the years," she says, "who wasn't able to rise to the occasion."

PREPARING FOR THE NEXT CENTURY

"I see a number of opportunities in it for the teens," says Ken Gimblin, a California high school teacher since 1960, who has long been active in helping students find volunteer jobs in government.

(Continued on page 68)

(Continued from page 67)

"First, there's experience in the area of government," notes Gimblin. "In a number of cases it has led to jobs. The second thing is, besides having a better understanding of government, it better equips them for the professional work world, which is critical. The third thing is, it gets them out into the community. I believe in academics, I believe in the classroom, but I think it's extremely important that students—and I'm sure this is why some of the school boards are asking for volunteer work—do get out into the community.

"Not only that, you're going to be a better person for it. And isn't that the whole goal of it?"

Gimblin "would like to see more of this done, not less," because he thinks that "as we enter the next century we're going to need to get students into the community even more than we're doing now."

Working in any government office can help you learn skills that you can apply in many different kinds of jobs. If you become computer-literate working in a government office, for example, you can transfer your competence to any number of office situations. And the same goes for your telephone etiquette, understanding of correct filing procedures, and people skills. The practical applications are almost limitless.

Beyond such nuts-and-bolts applications, you can expect to gain a hands-on understanding of government. If, like most of us, you expect to live your lifetime as a citizen in a representative democracy, you can acquire some firsthand perspective by sitting in on meetings of your city council, taking notes on calls from concerned constituents, drafting replies to angry or unhappy letters, or touring the back streets as well as the pleasant byways of an assembly district.

When they're filing and looking at the papers and all of the reports from committees, they can see why they're important and what the connection is. They get a flavor for the issues and problems that are out in the community, and how I might go about addressing them. It gives them a sense of what local government is all about.

—**Happy Haynes,**
Denver, Colorado, City Councilwoman

Take the two ninth-graders who created the website for the League of Women Voters. They became well aware of the relationship among levels of government. In gathering information and planning the website, they met the registrar of voters and other key people. They found they had to explain to their friends what they were doing and how the political process works. They started asking the LWV adults questions about polling places and how to vote and when to vote. They also wanted to know why the league would not allow them to become full members until they turned 18. When they learned that the league has a rule that you must be a U.S. citizen and 18 years old in order to be a full-fledged member, they thought that was a little unfair. And they questioned why it was called the League of Women Voters when it also has male members.

I can study government all I want in the classroom. I can memorize all the different rules for legislation, and the requirements to become a senator, but this was a chance for me to get my hands in there and work with the people—work with the constituents—and be a part of the process. That's something you can't do just sitting in a classroom. Making calls, being part of the process, is just an incredible feeling. This gives me a chance to see what it's really like.

—Melissa Colangelo, Teen Volunteer in
the New Haven, Connecticut, office
of U.S. Congresswoman Rosa L. DeLauro

If you serve on your city's youth commission, you are bound to get to know others' points of view as you work closely with them on whatever projects you are undertaking as a group. Bringing together a group of teens who don't know each other to work on a youth commission is not easy. As you are probably aware, closely knit groups of teen peers like to stick together and are often wary of strangers. But once teen volunteers who don't know each other get together on a project and see that it works, they realize how valuable it is to meet kids from other schools and other neighborhoods.

We tend to do everything in our neighborhoods—go to church, go to schools, hang out. It is fabulous that young people come together who don't know each other at all and we do have a cross section of the city youth—races, religions, economic class—everything.

—Nancy Gilder, Adviser to
the Denver, Colorado, Commission on Youth

(Courtesy: Denver, Colorado, Commission on Youth)

Teenagers who belong to youth commissions learn to interact with each other and build worthwhile friendships. These youth commissioners have just finished cleaning up a Denver, Colorado, park for a community-service project.

Another thing that makes the work interesting is the fact that you become "support staff" the instant you are given your first project. Your first assignment may be as simple as going to the copier to make duplicates of some letter or document or as ambitious as digging up extensive statistics from office records, other departments or even the public library.

Jordan Paul, high school senior and volunteer in the office of Connecticut State Senator Jim Fleming, says, "Volunteering in an office like this makes everyone happy. It's free labor for the senator and staff, and the volunteer gets a lot out of it, so there's no downside. They want some extra hands around here, and I want the experience. So if you make yourself available, they're likely to give you the opportunity."

A SENSE OF ACCOMPLISHMENT

There's one more thing in it for you. Your work as a volunteer in government is almost certain to leave you with a sense of accomplishment—in at least three different areas.

First, you will feel you are doing something significant for your community. You will be proud of the work that is done and your part in getting it done.

Second, you are also sure to improve the overall image of teenagers, both among the professional government workers who get to know you and see what you do and among the public—the constituents—whom you serve.

Third, you will gain in self-confidence. If you were self-confident before you started, you can expect to be even more so when you complete your tour of duty.

Johnnie Rodriguez, San Antonio Project Coordinator with the Southwest Voter Registration Project (SVREP), describes how he conducts a project roundup that produces this feeling. "At the end," he says, "we try and take the high school volunteers and give them lunch and then we tally up what we've done, how many total houses we contacted, how many live contacts there were, how many already were registered voters, how many new voters we registered, how many people pledged to go out and vote, how many absentee applications we filled out. That way, the teens can see just what they did. So by the time they get finished with this project, they get a sense of accomplishment."

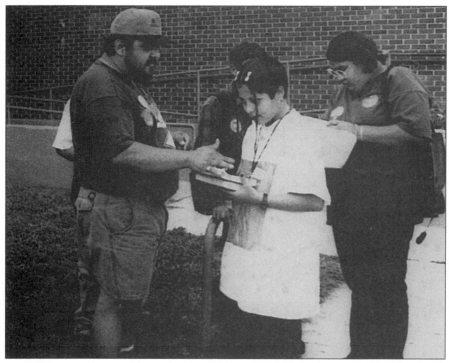

(Courtesy: Liz Trevino, Yearbook Staff/SVREP, San Antonio, TX)

Johnnie Rodriguez, coordinator for the Southwest Voter Registration Project, instructs Laura Cardenas (in T-shirt) before going house-to-house registering people to vote.

Trish Fontana, aide to the lieutenant governor of California and former high school volunteer, does something similar but in a one-on-one setting:

> A couple of days before they leave, I sit with each volunteer individually and ask about their first overall impression of the office. I might bring up something they did and were just terrified of, whether it was running the copier or meeting the lieutenant governor, and I'm amazed that they're able to really see their progress. I

enjoy seeing the way they start to perceive things differently. It's neat to see them grow, week by week, in front of you.

I just want them to walk away with a higher level of self-confidence or self-esteem. I want them to know that they can work in the adult world and not be considered a young kid who doesn't know how to do anything, but that we recognize them for the skills that they have.

Some teens come in real shy and walk out of here with the ability to get on the phone and call up the governor's office and demand action. It builds a lot of self-confidence. It did with me.

—Jim Fleming, Connecticut State Senator

CHAPTER FIVE

Is It Right for You?

*T*here are many advantages and satisfactions that you can get from volunteering in government and politics. There are also some disadvantages and dissatisfactions you may have to face. When you have reviewed some of these, you can take a self-quiz—a set of questions to help you decide if this area is right for you.

ADVANTAGES AND SATISFACTIONS

Perhaps the most satisfying aspect of this work is knowing that what you are doing is meaningful. That's what Melissa Colangelo found so rewarding—the fact that she was "part of the process."

Think about some of the advantages and satisfactions you can gain:

Handling Responsibility. In most of the situations described in this book, you get good practice in taking on responsibility. The very fact that you are working in an office that serves the public demands that you conduct yourself more professionally than you may have to in a typical after-school, weekend or summer job.

Gaining Recognition and Respect. With your voluntary service, you make new friends not only among your peers but also among the adult volunteers and staff people with whom you work. Getting their recognition and approval can be especially valuable. For example, they can help you when you need recommendations or references to put on college or job applications.

Making New Friends. Volunteering in any government office introduces you to new people beyond your usual group—those your own age, and others who are older or younger than you. You are almost certain to work with students who do not go to your school or live near you. Often you not only get the pleasure of bonding with them but you also make lifetime friendships.

Gaining School Credit. Your teachers and advisers will be glad to know of your service in government. You may get extra credit for it or even—depending on the policy of your local school board—course credit toward your high school diploma.

Gaining Relationships That Work. When you help staff people in an office, you build relationships that can bring rewards. Maybe you do an arduous photocopying job that's really a bore, but the staff person for whom you did it is likely to remember and to give you a task that is truly interesting another time.

GETTING AN INSIDER'S PERSPECTIVE

"The advantage I see," says Lela Young, an 11th-grader who volunteered in the office of the lieutenant governor of California, "is that you can actually get involved in it while you're there. You can go see what the legislature does while it's in session. You meet the other people. You see how the governor's office operates. You may never be there again, so you might as well take advantage of it and make the most of your experience. Consider

(Continued on page 77)

(Continued from page 76)

yourself the equal of everyone else who's working there.

"The most important thing I learned is not to be afraid to ask questions about what you're working on. At first I was nervous. If I was doing something wrong, I didn't want to admit it. But as I went along, I realized people are always making mistakes in what they do, and that's the only way you can learn."

Trish Fontana, who coordinates the work of teen volunteers in that office, started out by discovering the advantage of volunteering as a teen. "My high school government teacher made me do 15 hours in a campaign office," she says. "I didn't want to do that. But several years later, when I was hired here, I wrote a letter back to her and told her that she truly made the difference. Because it really is the exposure that you remember and take advantage of."

Fontana thinks of others who were able to find advantages they did not expect. "I watched an intern who was part of an Upward Bound program in Los Angeles," she recalls. "These are students who come from low-income families but have achieved academically high standards—yet they would not go on to college just because of finances and whatnot. This one student couldn't even talk the first week, she was so shy. This was a six-week program that she was in, about eight years ago. Now she's the policy person in the Speaker's office. And she's quite an advocate for the teen volunteer program. So it does impact students one way or another. And I'm not talking about them even going on to college."

On the other hand, adds Fontana, "one student got a full scholarship to Harvard, and he was a volunteer during the

(Continued on page 78)

(Continued from page 77)

summer. He's in contact with me, and comes to visit me every Christmas. He was at Oxford doing his master's degree, and he has been asked to start teaching. He's a homegrown Sacramento tomato boy here, and an exceptional student. I get e-mails from him every once in a while. He's just a remarkable young man, and there's a really great future for him."

I tell the teens as they go into various places, "I know you're going to be in awe of this but at the end of the semester you're going to feel that you can run the place." I think oftentimes that's true. The most important advantage is gaining the confidence, the experience of dealing with professional adults.

—Ken Gimblin, Teacher and Adviser
to Teen Volunteers in Sacramento, California

▼

You must have the self-discipline to adhere to a tight schedule.

DISADVANTAGES

There are some negative things you should think about:

No Pay. You must weigh the advantages you will get from a volunteer job against the disadvantage of giving up time that you could be using to earn money—especially once you are old enough to drive a car and go to a paying part-time job.

Time. When you make a commitment to be in a government office for several hours a week, you have to be able to balance your time, allowing enough for homework and for extracurricular activities and sports at school. You must have the self-discipline to adhere to a tight schedule.

Lack of Attention and Help. Most of the experiences of teen volunteers described in this book are quite positive. But you may find yourself in a situation in which no one is paying very much attention to you. The attitude seems to be, "O.K., here's what you do. Now go do it."

If you find that you are not being included on the team, you may soon become discouraged. It is one of the negatives to watch out for. If you do feel neglected, speak up about it. Tell your supervisor that you are capable of becoming more involved, and suggest projects where you can demonstrate your abilities.

Constituent Attitudes. One of the negatives you must face if you are dealing with phone calls and letters from the public is the fact that not everyone in this world is even-tempered or polite. When people get their dander up enough to complain to the mayor, a city council member or their state or U.S. representative, they sometimes forget that the person who takes the call or reads the letter is not the person responsible for the problem. If you're handling call intake and correspondence, you have to be oblivious to anger, insults and even name-calling.

Brian Wise, who spent the summer of 1997 as a volunteer in the office of the lieutenant governor of California, says, "I can honestly say there were some disadvantages. You're always going to miss some opportunities. One thing is, I'm very involved with Kiwanis International and the Special Olympics, and that's one of the things I missed, because I was up in Sacramento all summer and I wasn't able to go on a lot of the activities that they sponsored. And I do a lot of volunteering for Habitat for Humanity, and things like that, and I missed out on some of those, like helping to build a couple of houses. But the flip side was so great. I feel I fulfilled my civic duty."

One more disadvantage that Brian notes: He says that "a lot of times, a bad emphasis is put on teenagers. Like, right now, I'm 18. Well, if I talk to someone on the phone and they know my age, they automatically draw a picture of me, just because of the way the media portray teens. But I can tell you that at least half of the teenagers really are good people who are out there trying to improve society."

The only disadvantage is that sometimes people who call are screaming and yelling because they're upset about something the congresswoman supported, or they're unhappy with their current situation and they think it's the government's fault. It's sad when you know you can't help people. For example, the housing lists right now are incredibly long, and you get calls in from people who need public housing. But that's why we're there. We try and work on those things.

—Melissa Colangelo, Teen Volunteer
in the New Haven, Connecticut, Office
of U.S. Congresswoman Rosa L. DeLauro

SELF-QUIZ

How do you know whether you're right for the job? Here are some questions to help you decide about volunteering for government or political work.

- Are you interested in finding out how government works—at the local, state or national level?
- Are you the political or governmental type yourself? Do you like to be in charge, to be elected to office, to help run systems that organize people and guide their actions?
- Does the field of education appeal to you? Are you thinking of becoming a teacher?
- Can you speak to a classroom or assembly of schoolmates?
- Are you an organizer? A leader?

(Courtesy: Happy Haynes/Denver, CO)

Volunteering shows you care about the future of your community.
Happy Haynes, a member of the city council of Denver, Colorado,
provides youths with an opportunity to donate their services. Nikki
and Yvonne gained hands-on environmental experiences through
the Bluff Environmental Project (Bluff Lake, Denver) in 1997.

- Can you commit anywhere from 30 to 200 hours of the school year, or 50 hours of your summer, to this work?
- Can you balance your schoolwork, a paying job, this volunteer job and not "spread yourself too thin"?
- Can you ask questions? When you don't understand, are you willing to say so?
- Are you interested in helping your community?
- Are you willing to help save a staff person's time by doing the "gofer" work in an office today in order to get more interesting assignments tomorrow?

If you answered "yes" to a number of these questions, volunteering in government and politics may well be for you.

Where to Find Opportunities

Start your search by finding the names and office locations of your elected officials in local, state and national government. The blue pages of your telephone directory should have most of them, and the public library can help with the rest. Watch your local newspapers for information on these officials. Gather a file of clippings so you can look through them and select likely doors to knock on.

We send a letter regularly to area high schools inviting them to send students.

> —Heather Picazio, an aide in the
> Hartford, Connecticut, Office
> of U.S. Senator Joseph L. Lieberman

Call or stop in at the reference desk at your public library. Ask the librarian about such organizations as the League of Women Voters (LWV) and others that encourage voters to understand public issues and to register and vote. (The LWV "encourages people to contact the state presidents." See the appendix for a list of them.)

(Courtesy: M.S. Wirtenberg/LWV, Weston, CT)

The League of Young Women Voters (LYWV) is a good place to volunteer if you enjoy working with the public and want to learn more about public awareness. In Weston, Connecticut, The LYWV works with the League of Women Voters (LWV), cosponsoring such events as this Party for Democracy.

Network with your parents, relatives, friends, parents of friends, teachers and guidance counselors. They may already have contacts with elected officials and political organizations.

Sometimes a city council member may have been enjoying the advantages of using teen volunteers for some years while another member of the same city council has no such program. The same is true of the two U.S. senators from a given state, even though you would expect that senators from the same state would have similar programs. The fact that an office has not had teen volunteers in the past is no reason for you not to propose that it have them in the future. If you call an office and are told, "We don't use teen volunteers," it won't hurt to suggest that they start with you. Nothing ventured, nothing gained.

Don't be afraid to pick up the phone and call your legislator. Get hold of the legislator personally and say, "I'd like to work for you." Most legislators would love to have you. Be persistent. It doesn't require any special skills. You've just got to be able to read.
—Connecticut State Senator Jim Fleming

APPLICATIONS AND INTERVIEWS

When you call, ask for the person who coordinates volunteers. You may not get that person on the first call, because all coordinators are busy. Be sure to leave a message, with your name and phone number, saying you want to find out about volunteering. Ask if you need an application form and if the coordinator can mail you one. Or you may offer to stop by and pick up the form.

If no one calls back within a few days, call again. Do not get discouraged. Persistence pays off. If you have decided on a particular place where you want to volunteer, keep at it. You may find that they accept applications only at certain times or seasons of the year.

If you can't get in right away, ask to be placed on a waiting list. Be sure to write thank-you letters that follow up on your calls. While you're thinking of them, you want *them* to be thinking of you.

When you are interviewed, feel free to ask questions. What kind of training program will you have to go through? How many training meetings a week, for how many weeks? How many teen volunteers are in the program? Is there a period of probation, and how long is it?

Let your interviewer know that you have thought about your volunteering. Make him or her aware that you want to know what you are getting into in the same sense that he or she wants to know about you.

GET A RÉSUMÉ READY

Looking for a volunteer job is similar to looking for a paying job. You want to make the best possible impression. Handing a résumé to your interviewer makes two points:

That you have been somewhere and done something, and

That you know how to think about where you have been and what you have done.

Include your full name, address, age, grade in school and school activities (e.g., Key Club, drama club, sports teams, science club, 4-H Club, publications, etc.) on your résumé. If you have been elected to office in any student organization, or as a member of your school's student council, be sure to include those facts. And don't forget part-time jobs, from baby-sitting to delivering newspapers, from mowing lawns to shoveling snow. You want the reader of your résumé to see how well-rounded you are.

HOW DO YOU LOOK

Somebody said, "You get only one chance to make a good first impression." Dress for it, in clean, freshly pressed clothing. Make

(Courtesy: Bill Jones, secretary of state, Sacramento, CA)

Scott Jones (left) recognizes the importance of a neat appearance when volunteering as an intern for the secretary of state's office in Sacramento, California. Working with him are Alfie Charles, deputy communication director, and Shirley Washington, press secretary.

sure your hands and fingernails are clean. Your hair should be neat and clean. If it's long, make sure it's gathered away from your face. Make it clear you know you shouldn't come to work with your hair flying in the breeze.

A TASTE OF GOVERNMENT

If you want to get a taste of what it is like to participate in government before you actually volunteer, you might want to check out the Youth in Government program sponsored by the national YMCA organization. This is an extracurricular program for high school students that has been offered in schools in some three dozen states since the mid-1960s.

"We do a mock legislative process," says Kevin McCorry, director of communications at the YMCA of Metropolitan Denver in Colorado. "It starts with volunteer teachers at schools. They hold after-school sessions with the students to help them with bill writing as part of the legislative process. They just write their own bills, and then divide up into representatives and senators, lobbyists and press, and debate their bills and see if they can pass them through their own government."

In Colorado and in such states as California, Texas, and Virginia, says McCorry, the program is held in the state capitols and the chambers of the senate and representatives, as well as in various committee rooms. "That's so the teenagers can feel the depth and breadth of what it's like to be in politics and government," he notes. "We have elected officers. The governor of the state youth-in-government is an elected office, and the president of the senate and speaker of the house are also elected."

The Colorado program is so successful, according to McCorry, that it must run two programs simultaneously. It elects only one governor, but fills two houses of representa-

(Continued on page 89)

(Continued from page 88)

tives and two senates. "We have more than 400 teens participating," says McCorry, "with probably 25 to 30 high schools
from Colorado Springs up through Boulder."What happens
to the legislation written by the teens? At the conclusion of
the program, McCorry explains, if legislation has been voted
through the whole system, it is signed by the youth governor. It is then presented to the Colorado state legislature—to
the president of the senate and the speaker of the house—for
their review. "There have been bills throughout the country,"
says McCorry, "that have been presented to state legislatures
and have actually become law, and the teens were the impetus
for writing the legislation."

If you would like to find the YMCA Youth in Government
program nearest you, call 1 (800) USA-YMCA (i.e., 872-9622).
Ask the receptionist to connect you with someone who can
talk about the Youth in Government program.

GLOSSARY

Constituent. A member of a group that elects one of its members to represent the group in public office.

Federal. In the United States, a reference to the national government as a sovereign power.

Jurisdiction. The abstract limits or geographical territory over which an authority has power to govern.

Legislation. Laws or rules made by a government's legislature.

Legislature. The law-making branch of a government.

Nonpartisan. Not siding with any particular political party.

Notary public. A public officer who certifies the authenticity of writings, depositions and other matters for legal purposes.

Partisan. Siding with a particular political party.

Policy binder. A notebook containing statements of policy on various issues, for use by executives of an organization or government.

Political party. Any organized group that controls or seeks to control a government.

Press packet. Group of text materials and, usually, photographs prepared for distribution to members of the media, often at a press conference.

Private sector. Generally, business and other organizations that are not a part of a local, regional, state or national government.

Registration. Act of officially enrolling one's name as a prerequisite to voting.

Sovereign. An authority that enjoys supreme power.

SUGGESTIONS FOR FURTHER READING

The World Book Encyclopedia provides interesting articles on the related subjects of Government; United States, Government of the; State Government; City Government; Local Government; Legislatures; Political Party; Democracy; Bureaucracy; Election; and Town Meeting.

The following books will provide interesting reading on government and politics:

Bernotas, Bob. *The Federal Government: How It Works.* New York: Chelsea House, 1990.

Eichner, James A. and L.M. Shields. *Local Government* (revised edition). New York: Watts, 1983.

Liston, Robert A. *Getting in Touch with Your Government.* New York: Messner, 1975.

Raynor, Thomas P. *Politics, Power, and People: Four Governments in Action.* New York: Watts, 1983.

The following books will help give you a broad understanding of volunteerism and opportunities in community service:

Berkowitz, Bill. *Local Heroes: The Rebirth of Heroism in America.* Lexington, MA: Lexington Books (D.C. Heath), 1987.

Buckley, William F., Jr. *Gratitude: Reflections on What We Owe to Our Country.* New York: Random House, 1990.

Coles, Robert. *The Call of Service: A Witness to Idealism.* Boston: Houghton Mifflin, 1993.

Daloz, Laurent A., Cheryl H. Keen, James P. Keen and Sharon Daloz Parks. *Common Fire: Lives of Commitment in a Complex World.* Boston: Beacon Press, 1996.

Ellis, Susan J., and Katherine H. Noyes. *By the People: A History of Americans as Volunteers.* San Francisco: Jossey-Bass, 1990.

———. *The Volunteer Recruitment Book.* Philadelphia: Energize, Inc., 1994.

Grashow, Mark. *How to Make New York a Better Place to Live.* New York: City and Company, 1994.

Griggs, John, ed. *Simple Acts of Kindness: Volunteering in the Age of AIDS.* New York: United Hospital Fund of New York, 1989.

Lewis, Barbara. *The Kid's Guide to Service Projects.* Minneapolis: Free Spirit, 1993.

Luks, Allan, with Peggy Payne. *The Healing Power of Doing Good: The Health and Spiritual Benefits of Helping Others.* New York: Fawcett Columbine, 1991.

Olasky, Marvin. *Renewing American Compassion.* New York: The Free Press (Simon & Schuster), 1996.

Salzman, Marian, and Teresa Reisgies. *150 Ways Teens Can Make A Difference.* Princeton, NJ: Peterson's Guides, 1991.

Spaide, Deborah. *Teaching Your Kids to Care: How to Discover and Develop the Spirit of Charity in Your Children.* Secaucus, NJ: Carol Publishing Group, 1995.

Tarshis, Lauren. *Taking Off: Extraordinary Ways to Spend Your First Year Out of College.* New York: Fireside (Simon & Schuster), 1989.

Wuthnow, Robert. *Acts of Compassion: Caring for Others and Helping Ourselves.* Princeton, N.J.: Princeton University Press, 1991.

APPENDIX A

State Presidents of the League of Women Voters

STATE	PRESIDENT	TELEPHONE
Alabama	Anne Permaloff	(334) 277-1220
Alaska	Wilda Hudson	(907) 272-0366
Arizona	Lila Schwartz	(602) 997-5218
Arkansas	Bobbie E. Hill	(501) 376-7760
California	Karyn Gill	(916) 442-7215
Colorado	Marilyn Shuey	(303) 863-0437
Connecticut	Kristen Karpen	(203) 288-7996
Delaware	Jacqueline Harris	(302) 571-8948
District of Columbia	Luci Murphy	(202) 331-4122
Florida	Fay P. Law	(850) 224-2545
Georgia	Sara Clark	(404) 874-7352
Hawaii	Jean Aoki	(808) 531-7448
Idaho	Carol Woodall	(208) 883-5362
Illinois	Jan Flapan	(312) 939-5935
Indiana	Dalyte Hartsough	(317) 241-8683
Iowa	Mary Lange	(515) 277-0814
Kansas	Susan Holmes	(913) 234-5152
Kentucky	Betty Hilliard	(502) 875-6481
Louisiana	Malinda Hill-Holmes	(504) 344-3326
Maine	Sally Bryant	(207) 622-0256
Maryland	Joan Paik	(410) 269-0232
Massachusetts	Nancy Carapezza	(617) 523-2999
Michigan	Flora McRae	(517) 484-5383
Minnesota	Judy Duffy	(612) 224-5445
Mississippi	Kay Higginbotham	(601) 352-4616
Missouri	Carol Portman	(314) 961-6869
Montana	Ruth Centers	(406) 363-3734
Nebraska	Deanna Frisk	(402) 475-1411
Nevada	Celia Hildebrand	(702) 884-2659
New Hampshire	Lillian M. Nelligan	(603) 225-5344
New Jersey	Dorothy Dunfee	(609) 394-3303
New Mexico	Charlotte Zerof	(505) 982-9766
New York	Evelyn Stock	(518) 465-4162
North Carolina	Marian Dodd	(919) 783-5995
North Dakota	Lois Altenburg	(701) 772-7940
Ohio	Anne Smead	(614) 469-1505
Oklahoma	Carol Woodward	(405) 232-8683
Oregon	Paula Krane	(503) 581-5722
Pennsylvania	Mary F. Etezady	(717) 234-1576
Rhode Island	Hollie Courage	(401) 453-1111
South Carolina	Mary Ann Burtt	(803) 791-9044
South Dakota	Mina E. Hall	(605) 338-5525
Tennessee	Faye Johnson	(615) 297-7134
Texas	Julie Lowenberg	(512) 472-1100
Utah	Janice Gygl	(801) 272-8683
Vermont	Sonya Schuyler	(802) 657-0242
Virgin Islands	Debra Brown-Roumu	(802) 774-3106
Virginia	Connie Houston	(804) 649-0333
Washington	Elizabeth Pierini	(206) 622-8961
West Virginia	Ellender M. Stanchina	(304) 343-2706
Wisconsin	Kathryn Johnson	(608) 256-0827
Wyoming	Angeline Kinnaman	(307) 324-5460

Source: The League of Women Voters of the United States, 1730 M Street, NW, Suite 1000, Washington, DC 20036-4508. Phone: (202) 429-1965; Fax: (202) 429-0854; e-mail: lwv@lwv.org.